THE 10™

Most Revolutionary Inventions

Robert Cutting

Series Editor
Jeffrey D. Wilhelm

Much thought, debate, and research went into choosing and ranking the 10 items in each book in this series. We realize that everyone has his or her own opinion of what is most significant, revolutionary, amazing, deadly, and so on. As you read, you may agree with our choices, or you may be surprised — and that's the way it should be!

Franklin Watts®
an imprint of
SCHOLASTIC
www.scholastic.com/librarypublishing

A Rubicon book published in association with Scholastic Inc.

Ru'bicon © 2007 Rubicon Publishing Inc.
www.rubiconpublishing.com

Associate Publishers: Kim Koh, Miriam Bardswich
Project Editor: Amy Land
Editor: Dona Foucault
Editorial Assistant: Nikki Yeh
Creative Director: Jennifer Drew
Project Manager/Designer: Jeanette MacLean
Graphic Designer: Brandon Köpke

The publisher gratefully acknowledges the following for permission to reprint copyrighted material in this book.

Every reasonable effort has been made to trace the owners of copyrighted material and to make due acknowledgment. Any errors or omissions drawn to our attention will be gladly rectified in future editions.

"IM Slang Is Invading Everyday English" by Neda Ulaby, NPR, February 18, 2006. © 2005 National Public Radio, Inc.

"PCs by day, supercomputer by night" by George Butters and Stephen Butters, *The Globe and Mail,* June 19, 2006. Courtesy of George Butters and Stephen Butters.

"Reinventing the Wheel" from "Michelin Lets the Air Out of Future Tire Innovation," January 9, 2005. Permission courtesy of Michelin North America.

Cover image: Shutterstock

Library and Archives Canada Cataloguing in Publication

Cutting, Robert, 1952-
      The 10 most revolutionary inventions/Robert Cutting.

Includes index.
ISBN 978-1-55448-460-7

      1. Readers (Elementary) 2. Readers—Inventions. I. Title.
II. Title: Ten most revolutionary inventions.

PE1117.C975 2007   428.6   C2007-900542-X

1 2 3 4 5 6 7 8 9 10   10   16 15 14 13 12 11 10 09 08 07

Contents

Necessity Is the Mother of Invention ...

You may have heard that old saying before. In many cases, it's probably true. Recognizing a need, a resourceful inventor jumps in to create something to fill the gap. While some inventions are created after years of experimentation, many others can come about by accident. Some inventions improve the way we live, while others, such as weapons of war, can do us harm.

Every day, something new is invented. So, what makes one invention more revolutionary than the next?

In making our choices for this book, we looked for inventions that revolutionized the way we live. These inventions helped propel civilization from a hunting-gathering society to the modern technological age. We ranked these inventions based on the following criteria: the impact each had on the way of life at the time it was invented; how long it endured; whether it led to other ideas and inventions; and whether the item still has an impact today.

Turn the pages and think about what your life would be like if these items had not been invented. Then you be the judge:

What is the most revolutionary INVENTION? of all time

Before the invention of the bow and arrow, early humans had to get dangerously close to their prey to kill it.

D ARROW

WHEN: In the late Paleolithic period — 30,000 to 10,000 years ago

WHO: Unknown

EUREKA: The bow and arrow might be a simple technology today, but it was a revolutionary weapon in its time.

The bow and arrow was the first missile weapon in history. When it was invented, it beat the spear by a long shot! It became possible to kill bigger prey from a longer distance away. With the bow and arrow, hunting for food became easier and more efficient. This invention transformed the way of life of the hunters and gatherers of the late Paleolithic period.

The primitive bow was a long thin rod bent in an arc by the bowstring. The arrow was a slim straight shaft with a sharpened tip, called the arrowhead. In use, the arrow is fitted to the bowstring and drawn back, storing the energy of the pull. When this stored energy is released, it increases the speed of the arrow as it flies toward the target.

Before the invention of firearms in the 15th century, the bow and arrow was a powerful war weapon. The crossbow, first used in China in 341 B.C., was a short, powerful bow mounted in a stock and released by a trigger. It fired like a rifle. The English longbow made history at the Battle of Agincourt in 1415. It was almost as tall as a person and it could fire arrows a distance of 600 feet. Six thousand English soldiers defeated 50,000 French troops because they used the longbow and the French didn't. Now that's impressive!

arc: *curved line*

Some people still hunt with bows and arrows today. What are some of the reasons people might prefer this method of hunting?

THE BOW AND ARROW

AND THE POINT IS?

A little strength goes a long way! The physics of stored and released energy meant that a small person could hunt or fight with the same success as a big person. Anyone who was strong enough to pull back the bowstring could get the job done. The bow and arrow had a range double that of the thrown spear. It was a better weapon for hunting, which meant there was more food for the family. This also meant extra time for thinking up new ideas to make life better.

The bow and arrow was also a war weapon for thousands of years, popular among ancient Egyptian, Assyrian, Hun, and Mongolian warriors. Armies with skillful horse archers scored major victories. In the Middle Ages, soldiers in Europe used the longbow in their battles.

Quick Fact

In the 1960s, a burial site dating to between 12,000 and 4500 B.C. was found in ancient Nubia along the River Nile. Signs of arrowheads were found in the bones of four skeletons, and arrowheads were buried with many of the skeletons.

WHAT IF?

Without the bow and arrow, people would have to use primitive tools like spears and stones to kill small animals, all within a short throwing range. Hunting for food would take up lots of time and energy. Our early ancestors would have had to focus a lot of their time on basic survival. They would not have had time to develop new ideas, and might have remained as hunting and gathering societies.

Quick Fact

Archery has been an important part of Mongolian history. Mongols were unbeatable warriors because they could shoot while galloping on a horse at full speed.

Quick Fact

Legend has it that William Tell, an expert marksman with the crossbow in the 14th century, was forced to shoot an apple off the head of his son in order to win his own freedom. He split the fruit in half without any problems!

William Tell is about to shoot an apple off his son's head.

WHAT NOW?

The bow and arrow is still used for war and hunting by some indigenous groups in Africa and South America. However, its popular use today is in target shooting and sport hunting. Archery was a competition event in the Olympic Games from 1900 to 1920. It was brought back to the Olympics in 1972.

indigenous: *native to the region*

The Expert Says...

" The bow was a principal weapon in warfare until eclipsed by firearms in the 15th century; it is still the primary arm of aboriginal peoples today. "

— Lane Rogers, *Grolier Multimedia Encyclopedia*

aboriginal: *group of people who are the original inhabitants of a region*

BULL'S-EYE!

Think you could be the next William Tell? The following descriptive list could be the beginning of your path to archery excellence!

Luckily, for fans of Olympic archery, the sport was reintroduced in the 1972 games in Munich, Germany. A standard set of rules was put in place and many nations took part. Today, there are four events in Olympic archery — Men's Individual, Women's Individual, Men's Team, and Women's Team. In all four events, the distance from the archer to the target is 70 meters (230 feet).

Bow: Olympic archers use the recurve bow. This bow features limbs that curve away from the archers to increase power. Bows today are constructed of wood, fiberglass, and graphite. The average bow length is 6 feet for men and 5.5 feet for women.

Arrow: An archer uses an arrow slightly longer than his or her arm. The length of the modern arrow is from 24 to 31 inches. Arrows are made of either aluminum or carbon graphite. Aluminum arrows are more uniform in weight and shape, but graphite arrows fly faster.

Archer: Does an archer need strength and stamina? Well, the average draw weight of a man's bow is 50 pounds. It is 35 pounds for the woman's bow. In an Olympic tournament, the bow is lifted and drawn more than 312 times.

Archers need to be extremely accurate to hit the center of the target — the bull's-eye. For a 90-meter target (almost 300 feet), the 10-ring target face is just 12 centimeters (five inches) in diameter! Imagine standing on the goal line of a football field and hitting an apple under the opposite goalpost! Ready for a challenge, anyone?

---

draw weight: *amount of force needed to pull back the bow*

? Research primitive bows and arrows. Compare them to modern ones. What has changed? What has stayed the same?

Take Note

The bow and arrow scored big in history as a revolutionary hunting and war weapon. It helped to move early hunting and gathering societies beyond basic survival. But it is only relevant in sport hunting and target shooting today. For these reasons, the bow and arrow secures the #10 spot on our list of revolutionary inventions.

- Before the bow and arrow, hunters used spears to hunt their prey. What advantages would a bow and arrow give a hunter?

5   4   3   2   1

Where would the world be without reruns?
Just kidding. Stay tuned to find out why
TV is so revolutionary ...

WHEN: 1923

WHO: Vladimir Kosma Zworykin (Vlah-dee-meer Koh-zma Zwohr-kin), Philo Taylor Farnsworth (Fee-lo Tay-lore Farne-zworth), and John Logie Baird (John Lo-guee Bear-d)

EUREKA: Television connects the world and puts news and entertainment at our fingertips.

In the late 1940s, television became one of the most popular forms of entertainment in North America. It brought about TV dinners and introduced the idea of eating in front of the tube.

Here is how television works. A camera captures an event at the source. A transmitter converts the pictures and sounds and sends them out in the form of electrical signals. Your TV set receives them by way of cable, antennae, or satellite dish and converts them back into images and sounds. So you get to see your favorite show with the click of a button or a remote control.

Television was invented in the 1920s through the work of three men. Vladimir Kosma Zworykin invented the picture tube in 1924, John Baird demonstrated his first television system in 1926, and Philo Farnsworth made the first electronic television in 1927.

It was not until after World War II that television became a craze not unlike the Internet today. It opened up the world to its viewers and changed their lifestyle. Even today it continues to affect what people eat, how they dress, and what they think about many issues.

THE TELEVISION

Over 22,000 miles above Earth, satellites like this are sending TV signals to satellite dishes everywhere.

AND THE POINT IS?

It didn't take long for TV to become a powerful news and information medium. TV allowed viewers to watch important events as they were taking place. When Neil Armstrong made his historic landing on the moon in 1969, almost 600 million viewers around the world witnessed the moment. The camera and transmitter were on the moon, but the electrical signal traveled more than 180,000 miles to our homes. Today, many cable companies and satellite providers offer hundreds of channels. These channels can cover a wide range of specific topics — wrestling, pets, and anime, for example.

WHAT IF?

Without television, many people would have to listen to the radio or check the Web and newspapers for news. We'd have to actually leave the house to see movies and sports events. Many people in the TV and media industries, such as news anchors, TV reporters, producers, and technicians, would not have jobs. And VCR and DVD technology would not have been created.

WHAT NOW?

Today, television technology is switching from the cathode-ray tube (CRT) to LCD and plasma TV, which provide high quality viewing. TV sets are slimmer and lighter than ever before. Today's television screens can even be used as computer screens, thanks to digital technology. When you add the Web and sites like YouTube to the mix, the line between television and computers starts to blur.

Quick Fact

Home run! The first TV event to attract millions of viewers was a World Series baseball game in 1947. The game was played between the Brooklyn Dodgers and the New York Yankees.

The Expert Says...

" This instrument can teach, it can illuminate; yes, and it can even inspire. But it can do so only to the extent that humans are determined to use it to those ends. Otherwise, it is nothing but wires and lights in a box. "

— Edward R. Murrow, journalist

10   9   8   7

EYEWITNESS TO CHANGE

It may be called an "idiot box," but television has the power to change the world. Check out these event profiles ...

Nixon-Kennedy Debate

In 1960, the first televised debate between presidential candidates Richard Nixon and John F. Kennedy was aired. It revolutionized the way that politicians present themselves to the public. Before the TV debate, Nixon was leading in the polls, but all that changed after it was shown on TV. While Kennedy appeared at ease, Nixon came across as sweaty and nervous. Viewers thought that Kennedy won the debate. People who only listened to the debate on the radio thought that Nixon had won!

The Nixon-Kennedy debate was broadcast on September 26, 1960.

? How much TV do you watch? How has your lifestyle been affected by television?

An unknown protester tries to stop a line of tanks in Tiananmen Square on June 5, 1989.

Tiananmen Square Massacre

Beginning in April 1989, students, intellectuals, and labor activists in China staged protests against the Communist government. The largest demonstrations took place in Tiananmen Square in Beijing. On June 4, 1989, the Chinese government ended the demonstrations by bringing in the army. Soldiers fired on innocent demonstrators, killing up to 3,000 people. Western media broadcast reports to TVs around the world. The televised reports generated such negative reactions that even today the U.S. and the European Union still refuse to sell weapons to China.

Take Note

Television was a revolutionary invention. It shaped modern society and influenced how people see themselves and the world. It started a craze (like the Internet has today). However, TV is slowly losing its popularity, having to compete with other popular media, such as the Internet. In our opinion, the TV should take the #9 spot after the bow and arrow.

- Conduct a survey on television viewing among your friends. How much TV do they watch each day? What kinds of programs do they watch? How has TV viewing affected their schoolwork? How has it affected their social life? What would they do with their free time if there were no television?

Quick Fact

The average North American watches about four hours of television per day. By age 18, the average child has seen about 200,000 violent acts on television.

5   4   3   2   1

(8) LENSES

Without the lens, some people might not be able to read this book. But wait — there are many more world-changing ways to use the lens.

WHEN: At the end of the 1200s, with vast improvements made in the 1600s

WHO: Zacharias Janssen (Zak-ah-rye-ess Jann-ssen), Galileo Galilei (Gal-lih-lay-oh Gal-lih-lay), Alessandro della Spina (Aless-androh deh-la Spee-na), and Salvino degli Armati (Sal-vee-noh deh-glee Arr-mah-tee) all made major improvements to existing lenses.

EUREKA: The lens is used in eyeglasses, microscopes, and telescopes. All these inventions have affected the way we think and live and how we see the world.

Without light, sight is impossible. We can see an object because light reflects off its surface and travels to our eyes. But it wasn't until the late 13th century that people applied this knowledge to correct poor vision. Convex lenses were used to correct farsightedness. These lenses focus light and make things look bigger, as with a magnifying glass. In the 14th century, concave lenses were used to correct nearsightedness. They spread light out so that the image appears smaller.

When someone had the bright idea of fitting lenses into tubes, the microscope and telescope were invented. Zacharias Janssen invented the first microscope. Anton van Leeuwenhoek (Anne-tawn van Lay-ven-hook) was the first to study bacteria and living cells in blood with a microscope in 1660. The renowned Italian astronomer Galileo Galilei built his first telescope in 1619 and used it to discover distant objects in our solar system.

So, for the changes that lenses made in the lives of a countless number of people all over the world, they hold the #8 spot on our list.

---

convex: *having surfaces that bulge out*
concave: *having surfaces that cave in*

 Which invention involving lenses means a lot to you? Explain.

LENSES

AND THE POINT IS?

Lenses are behind many scientific inventions that have become important parts of our lives. Lenses introduced us to worlds that were invisible to the naked eye — the very far and the very tiny. If it weren't for Galileo, who made great improvements to the telescope, we might still think that everything in the solar system orbits around Earth. The invention of the microscope led to the discovery of bacteria, revealing a world of tiny organisms that can make us sick.

WHAT IF?

Without corrective eyeglasses, people with defective eyesight would not be able to see things and function normally. Without microscopes or telescopes, the world would not have made important advances in medicine, science, and astronomy. And we would not have the small, compact digital camera that is so cool. Without cameras, we would have no historical photos, places would be less safe, and the paparazzi wouldn't be able to invade Lindsay Lohan's privacy.

WHAT NOW?

Leeuwenhoek's microscope had a magnifying power of 270 times and was considered the best of its kind at that time. In 1926, the electron microscope was invented. This device could magnify a small object up to two million times by using beams of electrons. Electrons are tiny particles with negative charges of electricity found in all atoms. In 1957, a new kind of telescope — the radio telescope — was built when scientists discovered that stars and galaxies were sending out radio waves in deep space. The radio telescope uses a radio receiver and antenna to pick up these radio waves.

---

magnifying power: *way of measuring an optical system's ability to make an object appear larger; 270 times = 270 times larger than with the naked eye*

Quick Fact

Want to see planets around nearby stars in our galaxy? Your best bet is the world's most advanced optical telescope in Arizona's Mount Graham International Observatory. Optical telescopes detect light rays. They are usually built on mountains high above the ground and away from the bright lights of the city.

Galileo Galilei

? What is the first thing you would look for in the night sky if you had a powerful telescope?

The largest lenses in the world are found in domed telescopes like this one.

10   9   **8**   7   6

MILLION DOLLAR CRIME FIGHTER

Watch out Gil Grissom! This microscope might soon steal your place on CSI. Meet QEMSCAN — the electron-scanning microscope used to help police in England solve crimes. This high-tech microscope uses a focused beam of electrons, instead of just light, to scan a soil sample. Then a super-powerful computer analyzes the sample's unique mineral composition. The information QEMSCAN provides can link a suspect to a crime scene. Take a look at this fact chart *for more info.*

Check out these numbers to see why you can count on QEMSCAN to solve the crime ...

5 milliseconds: The time it takes for this microscope to analyze a sample. It rapidly scans an electronic beam over the sample and then analyzes the X-rays.

10: The number of murder investigations that the QEMSCAN is being used in (as of 2006)

2: The number of suspects who have been convicted so far thanks to this microscope

£500,000 (US$975,000): The price of one QEMSCAN microscope

Less than .04 inch: The size of the rock particles that the microscope can examine — these tiny rocks, or soil particles, can link someone to a crime if they are found on the suspect's shoe or car tire.

1970s: The decade when Australian scientists developed the QEMSCAN. Its most popular use is in helping the mining industry examine rocks to determine mineral content.

12,000: The number of mineral analyses QEMSCAN can perforn in one minute

The Expert Says...

" The invention of the telescope ... marked the birth of the modern scientific method and set the stage for a dramatic reassessment of our place in the cosmos. "

— Brian Greene, professor of physics and mathematics, Columbia University

Take Note

Lenses are #8 on our list. They have made it possible for us to see objects as far away as distant stars and to examine things as small as a virus. They have enriched our knowledge of space and the universe. For as long as we have a need to see things better, lenses will continue to be important in our lives.
- In what ways have any of these inventions affected you personally: contact lenses, eyeglasses, binoculars, telescopes, microscopes, digital cameras, camcorders, and movie projectors? Are there any improvements you'd like to make to any of these?

5 3 2 1

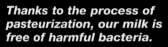

Thanks to the process of pasteurization, our milk is free of harmful bacteria.

...ION

WHO: Louis Pasteur (Lou-wee Pass-tehr)

EUREKA: The invention of pasteurization — heating foods to kill harmful organisms — brought about important advances in the medical world and saved lives.

In the past, people drank milk within hours after it was collected from cows or goats. Without reliable refrigeration the milk would have gone sour and germs would have multiplied.

In the mid-1800s, Louis Pasteur made a groundbreaking discovery. Using the latest microscopes, he saw thousands of tiny microbes (bacteria) swimming in milk. If people had known what lurked in even one drop of untreated milk, they might not have been so quick to drink it!

Pasteur proved that these microbes either existed in the cows or were introduced during bottling. So, he invented a way of killing the microbes without harming the milk. He heated liquid to a temperature of about 160°F to destroy harmful bacteria. This process was called pasteurization.

Pasteur was also the first scientist to prove that germs caused diseases. He believed that killing the germs would wipe out diseases. To kill the germs, he placed surgical instruments in high temperatures before use. Soon, hospitals around the world were using Pasteur's method of sterilizing medical instruments used in operations.

For its outstanding contribution to the medical world, Louis Pasteur's invention is #7 on our list.

PASTEURIZATION

AND THE POINT IS?

Pasteur's invention prevents milk from turning sour. Before pasteurization, milk went bad within a few hours, even when refrigerated. Now milk stays fresh for weeks. His discovery not only helped to make foods safer but also served as proof of the germ theory of disease. Before Pasteur, many scientists thought that germs appeared out of nowhere, leaving people with no way to prevent infections and contagious diseases.

WHAT IF?

Before pasteurization, the best way to get rid of bacteria was to boil all food. But boiling usually makes things taste awful (and removes nutrients!). The genius of the pasteurization process is that it heats the food just enough to kill all the bad bacteria and enzymes without drastically changing the taste.

contagious: *can spread to others*
enzymes: *proteins that speed up the rate of chemical reactions*

WHAT NOW?

Pasteur's discoveries were so important that funds were raised to start the Pasteur Institute in 1887. The institute, which is located in Paris, conducts research into infectious diseases. It has made breakthrough discoveries in controlling diseases such as diphtheria, tetanus, tuberculosis, influenza, and the plague. To Pasteur's credit, the pasteurization process is still used in every kind of food manufacturing today.

Louis Pasteur: founder of the germ theory of disease and inventor of pasteurization

? What dairy products are supposed to be sour or moldy? Why do you think it's okay for those products to be sour or moldy?

Quick Fact

Although the benefits of pasteurization are undisputed, some people believe that milk's nutrients and infection-fighting benefits are destroyed through pasteurization. The debate has made it into the courts because it is illegal to sell raw milk in Canada and many parts of the United States.

The Expert Says...

" Good sanitation ... [does] not eliminate the possibility of disease-causing bacteria. ... Drinking unpasteurized or raw milk or eating other dairy products made from raw milk has its risks. "

— Suzanne Driessen, food science educator, University of Minnesota

? Why do you think there is such a controversy over letting people drink raw milk? Is it just about the germs? Who would lose, or gain, if raw milk were allowed on all supermarket shelves?

10   9   8   7   6

Portable Pasteurization Could be Key for Developing Nations

A hot water bottle that could save the world? This account will make you a believer!

According to the World Health Organization (WHO), more than 2.6 billion people — that's more than 40 percent of the world's population — do not have basic sanitation. And more than one billion people still use unsafe sources of drinking water.

Solar Solutions, a company based in San Diego, California, has created a cheap, portable, solar pasteurization device that will purify water that might be contaminated with harmful water-borne bacteria and pathogens.

How it works:
The AquaPak is shaped like a big thermal food bag. Using only sunlight, it can heat water to temperatures higher than 153°F, killing bacteria, viruses, and parasites. The bag can be placed in the sunshine on car roofs, windowsills, thatched roofs, and people's backs as they work. An indicator lets the user know when the AquaPak has reached 153°F, a temperature that must be kept for about 15 minutes. One AquaPak can pasteurize up to four gallons of water per day, enough to keep a family of four healthy.

So far, Solar Solutions has distributed the AquaPak to 27 nations including Kenya, Malawi, and Nigeria.

The AquaPak™

pathogens: *things that cause disease*

Quick Fact

The heat is on! These days the most common method of pasteurization in the U.S. is High Temperature Short Time (HTST) pasteurization. It involves heating the milk to at least 161°F for 15 seconds. To give milk an even longer shelf life, manufacturers use Ultra High Temperature (UHT) pasteurization, which heats the milk to 280°F for two seconds.

Take Note

Pasteurization takes the #7 spot on our list. In our opinion, Pasteur's invention is even greater than lenses because it helps keep food safe and saves lives. Pasteurization has proved its effectiveness and will continue to play a major role in food processing and manufacturing.

• Since 1908, eight Pasteur Institute scientists have been awarded the Nobel Prize for medicine and physiology. Go online to research any one of these winners.

physiology: *science that deals with living organisms and their parts*

3   2   1

The steam engine is what's powering this train, but it also has many other life-changing uses!

571

STEAM TRAIN–SHUTTERSTOCK

ENGINE

WHEN: 1698, 1712, 1769

WHO: Thomas Savery (Say-voh-ree), Thomas Newcomen (New-come-ehn), and James Watt

EUREKA: The steam engine uses highly compressed steam (gas that results from boiling water) to create force to move vehicles or industrial machinery.

Thanks to the steam engine, we don't have to rely on animals, wind, water, or our own muscles for power! The steam engine was the first technology that allowed us to burn fuel for power. This engine actually turns steam into a mechanical force. When burning coal or oil, heat is produced and steam rises from the water inside a boiler. The steam pushes a piston, which sets off a motion that exerts energy.

Many inventors helped develop the steam engine. In 1698, English engineer Thomas Savery built a device that pumped steam into mines. Then in 1712, Thomas Newcomen built the first steam engine. It exerted a powerful up-and-down movement and was used for pumping water from coal mines. It was in 1769 that James Watt created the modern steam engine.

Starting in the late 18th century, the steam engine was used to power factory equipment, such as spinning machines and lathes. Steam power was later used for locomotives and steamships. The invention of the steam engine sparked the Industrial Revolution and brought major changes to the lives of people.

---

exerts: *puts to use*
lathes: *machines for shaping wood, metal, and other materials by rotating the material against cutting tools*

THE STEAM ENGINE

AND THE POINT IS?

People had long been fascinated by the idea of creating big machines that could be used to do lots of work. The steam engine made this possible. It also spawned many new inventions in the late 1700s, such as the steamship, the train, and cars. The steam engine revolutionized many things from transportation to industrial production.

WHAT IF?

Without the steam engine, the Industrial Revolution that started in the late 18th century wouldn't have occurred when it did. There would have been no machines in factories and no assembly lines. The social, cultural, and economic changes that followed would not have taken place.

? What do you think life was like before the Industrial Revolution? Do some research online.

James Watt's first rotary steam engine

WHAT NOW?

Thomas Savery, Thomas Newcomen, and James Watt all helped to create a perfect machine that operated on steam. They based their machines on work originally done by Denis Papin. He was the French innovator who invented a steam cooker in 1679.

? Why do you think steam engines stopped being popular? How would the world be different today if we had not relied on gas to power our vehicles?

The Expert Says...

"Watt realized that the problem with the model Newcomen engine was that it was hopelessly inefficient; masses of coal had to be burned to generate enough steam for just a couple of strokes."

— Adam Hart-Davis, chemist/broadcaster

FULL STEAM AHEAD

Steam can power just about anything. Check out this descriptive list for proof!

MANHATTAN, NEW YORK

Most people don't know this, but New York City is the world's largest consumer of steam power. In Manhattan, steam is used to power many buildings. It heats and cools the Metropolitan Museum of Art, the United Nations building, and Rockefeller Center. The city uses seven steam-generating stations to make about 14 million tons of steam power each year.

STEAM CATAPULTS

These are devices used to help planes take off on short runways on aircraft carriers. A steam catapult uses steam power. It is made up of two rows of slotted cylinders in a trough under the flight deck. Pistons inside these cylinders are connected to a shuttle that tows the aircraft.

> **?** Although nuclear power is a relatively clean energy source, health and environmental concerns relating to radiation exist. What action would you take if you learned that a nuclear power plant was to be built in your city?

BMW TURBOSTEAMER

BMW is developing a new technology that will recycle exhaust gases and turn them into steam. This system will give the engine 15 percent more power. More than 80 percent of the heat energy contained in the exhaust gases would be recycled using this technology.

NUCLEAR POWER

About 17 percent of the world gets their electricity from nuclear power plants. This process uses uranium power, an extremely high-energy source of heat. Energy is released when atoms of uranium are split. This is similar to what happens with an atomic bomb. But in a nuclear power plant, the release of energy is controlled. The high energy heats water, turning it into steam. The steam powers a steam turbine, which then spins a generator to produce power.

The steam catapult can help an aircraft reach speeds of over 120 mph in less than two seconds!

Take Note

Pasteurization, at #7 on our list of great inventions, was an important life-saving invention. But the steam engine helped to start off the Industrial Revolution, which had a major impact on the whole world. Living conditions improved, and people enjoyed a better standard of living as a result of economic, social, and cultural changes.
- Do you agree that the steam engine should hold the #6 ranking? Give reasons to support your opinion.

5　　**4**　　**3**

An example of Johannes
Gutenberg's original
printing press

PRESS

WHEN: 1440s

WHO: Johannes Gutenberg (Yo-hahnn Goo-ten-burg)

EUREKA: Gutenberg invented reusable metal movable type — this revolutionized printing and led to the spread of knowledge through reading.

Before printing was invented, books were so rare that they were chained to library walls. Every copy of every book had to be written out by hand. In the 6th century, printing was done using wood blocks. These were carved, covered in ink, and pressed onto paper. This method was good for single documents, but it was too slow and impractical for printing books.

In the 1040s, Pi Sheng of China invented movable type — single letters carved on small individual blocks. He used clay, which was not a durable material. It wasn't until the 1440s that Johannes Gutenberg perfected Pi Sheng's movable type. Gutenberg used cast and molded metal for each letter, number, and punctuation mark. He combined hundreds of movable letters to lay out a page. Once a page was printed, he simply recombined the letters for another page. He did not have to recarve each type as early inventors did. This was movable type printing, and it allowed Gutenberg to print books. He could also make many copies of a book easily.

Printing presses rapidly spread throughout Europe. Gutenberg's movable type printing press created an information revolution.

THE PRINTING PRESS

AND THE POINT IS?

Before Gutenberg's invention, very few books were produced. Books were mainly for priests and scholars who controlled knowledge and the flow of printed information. Once Gutenberg perfected the printing press, books became available and people learned to read. This led to the spread of knowledge and affected the way people thought about things.

WHAT IF?

Without the printing press, there would not have been the spread of knowledge through books. There was an explosion in learning, art, and culture in the period known as the Renaissance.

Quick Fact

When printed books were gaining in popularity, some nobles refused to have them in their libraries, believing that to do so would cheapen their valuable hand-copied manuscripts.

WHAT NOW?

Today, practically all movable type printing is based on Gutenberg's invention. However, with the advance in computer technology, printing houses are changing to digital presses. Printing machine operators are required to have computer skills. Operators monitor the printing process on a computer monitor and adjust the press electronically. The invention of compact computer printers has made printing documents a breeze.

Gutenberg and his press

Quick Fact

Gutenberg was able to print 1,000 Bibles per year with his press. In those days the Bible sold for 30 florins each, or the equivalent of three years of a person's wages at the time.

Why do you think people were willing to spend this much money on a Bible?

The Expert Says...

" The history of printing is an integral part of the general history of civilization. "

— Sigfrid H. Steinberg, in *Five Hundred Years of Printing*

integral: *essential; necessary*

What other inventions could be called "integral" to our history?

10   9   8   7   6

The Printing Press Comes of Age

From movable type to digital printers, this timeline has it all.

Roman empire to pre-1450: Illuminated manuscripts (handwritten books decorated and illustrated with gold leaf)

gold leaf: *gold beaten into a very thin sheet*

Late 1440s: Metal movable type press (hand operated)

1539: First printing press started operation in North America (in Mexico City)

1811: Steam-powered press (automated; 400 pages per hour)

1886: Linotype, a keyboard-operated machine (automated)

1903: Offset press (photo impression on the plate is printed to a rubber blanket and then to paper; can produce up to 500,000 impressions per hour or about 12 magazine pages per impression)

1990s: Laser printers and computer publishing software for home computers

An example of movable type set in a press

Original linotype machine

Example of a modern offset press ready to print!

Quick Fact

The heaviest newspaper ever was the September 12, 1987, edition of *The New York Times*, which weighed 12 pounds and had 1,612 pages.

Take Note

The steam engine, at #6, quite literally powered the Industrial Revolution. However, the printing press allowed for the spread of knowledge, which greatly influenced the course of history. Today, we have the ability to transmit and store knowledge digitally, but printed material will likely remain a part of our lives for years to come.

• Which invention do you think is more important — the steam engine or the printing press? Explain how they have affected your life.

5 **4** **3** **2** **1**

④ THE ALPHABET

According to the editors at the Oxford English Dictionary, there are at least a quarter of a million distinct English words (all this just from 26 little letters).

WHEN: Around 2000 B.C.

WHO: Ancient Sumerians and Egyptians

EUREKA: The alphabet is a standard set of letters or characters representing sounds used for writing a language. It became the means of communicating thoughts or information in a written form.

The cuneiform script of pictures was one of the earliest forms of written expression. It made use of drawings to express ideas. Another form of written expression was Egyptian hieroglyphics. Both of these early forms of writing involved learning thousands of pictures or symbols. It was not something that everyone could do.

The alphabet was invented in Mesopotamia (the land between the Tigris and Euphrates rivers, or modern Iraq) sometime around 2000 B.C. The alphabet quickly replaced the cuneiform script and hieroglyphics and simplified writing like never before. The Greeks added vowels to their alphabet sometime around the 5th century B.C. The Romans added punctuation and created a 23-letter alphabet. But they did not have the letters J, V, or W. These were added later to become the Roman alphabet that we know and use today. More than 1.9 billion people in the world use the 26-letter version of the Roman alphabet for written communication.

cuneiform: *wedge-shaped characters*
hieroglyphics: *symbols and pictures*

Example of how a representational picture of something could evolve into a letterform

THE ALPHABET

AND THE POINT IS?

Finally, just a few letters could be arranged in so many ways to describe everything from objects and places to emotions and time. Until the first alphabet was invented, it was hard to communicate with someone without actually being there in person. Figuring out a writing system paved the way for books and the sharing of knowledge. Written communication has helped to spread learning. It is also a convenient way to maintain a relationship with someone that you cannot talk to or meet in person.

> **?** What other inventions in this book have contributed to literacy and the easy exchange of ideas?

WHAT IF?

In the past, scientists had considered writing as one of the indications of civilization. Writing systems appeared to develop in agricultural and urban cultures. Writing was used for counting agricultural products and for keeping records. It was also used for keeping the calendar to plant crops at the correct time. Without the alphabet to simplify writing, our ancestors would have had a tougher time passing information and knowledge to future generations.

Ancient writing tools

> Have you ever played the broken telephone game? What happens to information when it is passed along orally through many people? **?** →

WHAT NOW?

Writing provides a way of extending what we can store in our collective memory. Without writing, our ideas and knowledge cannot be recorded and stored. Information might be forgotten and lost forever. And inventions like the printing press, the computer, the Internet, and text messaging would not have taken place.

Egyptian hieroglyphs

Cuneiform on a clay tablet: the earliest known form of writing

The Expert Says ...

" Ears are uncertain messengers to the treasury of memory. "

— Samuel Hartlib, in *The True and Ready Way of the Latin Tongue*, 1654

IM Slang Is Invading Everyday English

Report by Neda Ulaby

National Public Radio, February 18, 2006

☺ If you use instant messaging on your computer, you may be familiar with the acronym LOL (Laughing Out Loud). But what about BRB, TTYL, or ROFL? Especially among teenagers, you're just as likely to encounter IM-speak in the real world as you are on your desktop.

☺ Instant Messaging (IM) technology was popularized by AOL [America Online] during its rocketing rise in the 1990s. Now, it has spread to other systems such as Yahoo Messenger, MSN Messenger, and Google Talk.

Experts predict that by the year 2010 we will have sent 2.3 trillion text messages.

☺ Teens admit that some purists might read the advent of IM slang into speech as a negative development. But linguistics professor David Crystal thinks it is an enhancement. Instant message expressions have done more than just added to constructions of the English language and the roughly 200,000 words in common use today. "They extend the range of the language, the expressiveness ... the richness of the language," he says.

linguistics: *scientific study of language*

? Give examples of e-mail or instant messaging slang that you have used with your friends. Create a glossary of slang and invite your friends to add to it.

☺ The phenomenon of written IM slang crossing over into speech is manna for linguists. Professor David Crystal, who has written extensively on language and the Internet, observes: "I see a brand new variety of language evolving, invented really by young people ... within five years! It's extraordinary."

manna: *unexpected bonus*

Take Note

Without the alphabet, people would not be able to write and communicate as quickly and easily. The alphabet had to exist before there was a need to invent a printing press. Based on our argument, we give the alphabet the #4 ranking on our list.

- Compare the advantages and disadvantages of using written and spoken forms of communication at school and at home.

5   **4**   3   2   1

In the mid-1970s, the first personal computers had one kilobyte of memory — they wouldn't even be able to handle one of today's MP3 files (a four-minute song is about 4,000 kilobytes).

COMPUTER

WHEN: 1974

WHO: Ed Roberts and Les Solomon

EUREKA: The PC was a knockout! It replaced the mainframe — heavy, huge, inefficient, and expensive — and took us into the Information Age.

The personal computer has become such a big part of our daily lives. And yet it's the newest of all the 10 most revolutionary inventions in this book. How did we manage without it and how did it come about?

It was not so long ago that Ed Roberts and Les Solomon created the first personal computer (PC). It was called the Altair 8800, and the first model in 1974 came as a do-it-yourself kit. It was considered too difficult to assemble, and it sold only 1,000 units in the first year. Today, 130 million personal computers are sold each year!

Thanks to the microchip, the development of the PC took off later in the 1970s. The PC became more efficient and affordable. Soon it became a feature in almost every office, store, and home. In the 1990s, the popularization of the Internet and the World Wide Web shrank the world. The PC and computer technology will continue to affect the way we live, work, learn, and interact with others. For linking up the world and playing such a big part in our lives, the personal computer comes in at #3 on our list.

Think about how the PC has affected your life. How important is this invention compared to the ones you have read about so far?

THE PERSONAL COMPUTER

AND THE POINT IS?

The PC allows us to store and retrieve information for office work and school assignments. It also enables us to interact with friends, shop online, do research, listen to music, read books, and even watch movies. And we can do all these things instantly, 24 hours a day. Advances in nanotechnology have resulted in smaller and more powerful home computers and laptops.

nanotechnology: *art of building microscopic devices*

This PC from 1980 cost US$900 and only held four kilobytes of information!

Quick Fact

The first all-electronic computer was ENIAC (Electronic Numerical Integrator And Computer). When it was completed in 1946, ENIAC weighed 30 tons and filled a 30-by-30-foot room. The computer had 18,000 vacuum tubes that were used to perform calculations at a rate of 5,000 additions per second.

WHAT IF?

Without the PC, the Internet explosion would not have taken place. There would be no online chatting and e-mail, no online banking and learning, no e-commerce, and no desktop publishing. We would have to do things the old-fashioned way — write letters, make phone calls, go to the bank, visit the stores, read the newspapers, and submit handwritten reports.

WHAT NOW?

Tim Berners-Lee invented the World Wide Web in 1991. By 2003, 170 million computers were connected to the Internet — allowing for the viewing of text, graphics, and video. Experts predict that in the future, billions of devices will be connected. One of the growing concerns about the Internet of the future is: who will control all of this?

Quick Fact

Believe it or not, the first computers were inspired by an invention in the early 1800s! Joseph M. Jacquard invented a punch tile system to automate patterns in loom weaving. This technology was a very primitive version of how the first punch-card computers were programmed. The pattern of the punched holes would tell the loom (and later the computer) what to do.

This is just one room of the ENIAC computer.

PCs BY DAY, SUPERCOMPUTER BY NIGHT

An article by George Butters and Stephen Butters
The Globe and Mail, June 19, 2006

The students who use the computer lab at St. Francis Xavier University in Antigonish, NS, probably aren't aware that at night the lab transforms into the equivalent of a supercomputer. ...

At 11, the students are gone, the doors are locked, and the lights are out. It's time to close Windows until morning.

The workstations begin to automatically shut down. But about 400 of them are soon back up and running a GNU/Linux operating system as one big connected cluster of processing power — a grid computer.

A grid is a network of PCs controlled by special software that can offer the collective number-crunching power of a dedicated supercomputer. ...

In basic terms, grid software can take a massive computing job and split it into small chunks that each desktop machine on the network can process. The software then takes the results and reassembles them into a finished job, whether it's the answer to a complex physics problem or the creation of a climate-change computer model. ...

> **?** The computer, the television, and the Internet are three things belonging to the information technology revolution. Which do you value most and why?

The Expert Says...

" The remarkable rise of the personal computer ... has placed cheap computing power on desks in homes, offices, and schools. The personal computer has thus unexpectedly become the basic building block of the information technology revolution. "

—Tom Forester, editor of *The Information Technology Revolution*

Take Note

The personal computer is #3 on our list. It is less than 40 years old. Yet its impact on our society has been far-reaching. It is a product of the information technology revolution, which has changed the world in the 20th century and beyond. Computer technology affects all aspects of our life today and will continue to shape our future.

- There are often downsides to many great inventions — including the personal computer. Which invention in this book has the biggest drawbacks?

5   4   **3**   2   1

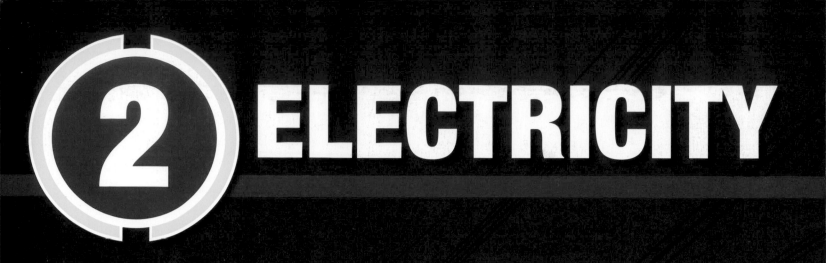

② ELECTRICITY

A massive blackout on August 14, 2003, gave
more than 50 million people in North America
a taste of life without electricity.

WHEN: Electricity exists in nature, but it wasn't until 1752 that this was proven.

WHO: Benjamin Franklin, Thomas Edison, Nikola Tesla, and many others contributed to the invention of technologies that harnessed the power of electricity.

EUREKA: Today we are more dependent on electricity than ever before. It powers our world and makes things run — from lightbulbs to computers.

Benjamin Franklin pulled a daring stunt in 1752. As the story goes, he wanted to prove that lightning was the same thing as static electricity. He attached an iron key to the end of a kite's string and held on to it during a thunderstorm. When lightning struck, a tiny spark jumped from the key to his knuckle. This could have killed him, but he did prove his point.

It didn't take long for other inventors to figure out how to use electricity to power buildings, homes, and household appliances. In 1800, Italian physicist Alessandro Volta built the electric battery. It provided the first continuous source of electricity. In 1879, Thomas Edison perfected the first practical long-lasting lightbulb. The demand for incandescent light became so huge that Edison quickly built the first power station to supply electricity. In 1882, he brought light and electric power to customers in Lower Manhattan, New York. His commercial power station was the first in the world.

Electricity has fed our consumer-driven society a cheap, safe, and reliable source of power since the 18th century. It has affected every aspect of the way we live and changed the life of almost every human being on this planet!

incandescent: *bright light from a hot source such as a bulb*

Which inventor in this book has most inspired you and why? Research this person and present a summary profile highlighting his invention.

POWER LINES–SHUTTERSTOCK

ELECTRICITY

AND THE POINT IS?

Before electricity, the streets were dark. People used gas and oil lanterns and fires to light up their homes. They relied on ice to refrigerate their food and woodstoves to heat their homes. Our lives changed when electric energy could be harnessed to power our machines, appliances, and gadgets. Electric power has revolutionized the way we live, making our lives comfortable, fun, and more efficient than ever before.

WHAT IF?

Without electricity, life would be very different. Luxuries like televisions, stereos, refrigerators, electric stoves, microwaves, and computers wouldn't even exist. And we would have to work harder to warm ourselves, cook our food, and wash our clothes without modern electric appliances.

> What are the three most important modern inventions in your life now? What benefits have they provided? What improvements would you make if necessary?

WHAT NOW?

Electricity is transmitted to consumers through overhead power lines. Are these high-voltage lines a health hazard? There is no conclusive evidence that they pose an increased risk of cancer. However, there are attempts to bury new power lines underground. Urban centers around the world thrive on electric power, but some developing countries still depend on wood, dung, and crop residue as fuel sources.

Quick Fact

Electricity travels at the speed of light — that's more than 186,000 miles per second!

Quick Fact

The volt is a unit used to measure electricity. It is named after Alessandro Volta. The common voltage of an AC power line is 120 volts. A spark of static electricity can measure up to 3,000 volts. A bolt of lightning can measure up to 3,000,000 volts!

DANGER HIGH VOLTAGE

10   9

A SHOCKING CHOICE

This account reveals the electrifying beginnings of our #2 invention …

Believe it or not, one of the first things that electricity became popular for was the electric chair!

In the mid-1880s, the New York State government started to look into an alternative to hanging as capital punishment. At the same time, the rivalry between Thomas Edison and his direct current (DC) electricity and Nikola Tesla's alternating current (AC) service was growing.

Edison said in public that AC was dangerous. In 1887, he used an AC generator attached it to a metal plate and executed animals by placing them on the electrified metal plate. The press went nuts over the event, and the term "electrocution" was coined.

direct current: electricity that flows in one direction (batteries only produce direct current)

alternating current: electricity that reverses direction many times per second (this is the type of power used in homes)

In 1888, New York State decided that it would look into using the electric chair as a new way to carry out capital punishment. But they had to decide what would be used — AC or DC? Edison publicly pushed for AC power to be used in the electric chair. Why? He had a lot of money invested in DC power and if people knew AC was used to kill people, they wouldn't want it in their homes.

Edison won the electric chair battle. However, his victory was short-lived. It soon became clear that AC service was better suited to supplying electricity to homes because DC power starts to lose its strength after traveling a mile or so. Alternating current is now used around the world.

Quick Fact

Tesla created the electric grid — a system of towers and transmission wires — to supply electricity over long distances.

Take Note

Although the personal computer, at #3 on our list, plays a big part in our daily lives, it would not function without electricity. We use more electric power than any other source of energy in our homes, schools, offices, and industries. It would be hard to function in our modern world without a constant supply of electric power.

• About 1.5 billion people around the world still lack access to electricity. How do you think these people's lives are different from yours?

The Expert Says…

"Electricity is the key that opened the door to all other inventions. Without electricity the world would, literally, still be in the dark ages."

— John Amey, *Triumph of Technology*, BBC

5   4   3   **2**   1

The wheel is used in everything from transportation to technology to toys — it definitely makes the world go around!

WHEN: About 3500 B.C.

WHO: There is evidence that the Sumerians were the first to use the wheel.

EUREKA: This simple device moves in a circular motion and was first used for transportation. It has endured through the ages and continues to have an impact on our lives today.

The wheel has to be the most important mechanical invention of all time. It's hard to imagine any mechanized system that works without the wheel or a rotating motion that transfers power along a circular path. We see it in the roller coaster and Ferris wheel, in tiny watch gears, and in computer disk drives. And we know there are gears inside our car engines and other heavy machines.

The wheel started out as a wooden disk with a hole for the axle. After two wheels were attached to the axle, wooden carts were placed on top, and heavy loads could be moved quickly. It was the beginning of transportation. And it led to other significant developments in history, such as the waterwheel, cogwheel, and spinning wheel.

The Sumerians set the wheel in motion. Today, we are a long way from the wooden-wheeled chariots, two-wheeled farm carts, and four-wheeled freight wagons of long ago. The wheel has become the central component of technology in almost all our mechanical and electronic inventions. We recognize the wheel for its enduring quality, its inescapable influence, and its impact on our lives. It is our choice for the #1 spot on our list.

---

waterwheel: *wheel driven by water to run machinery or raise water*
cog wheel: *wheel with a series of teeth on the edge*
component: *part of a mechanical system*

THE WHEEL

AND THE POINT IS?

The invention of the wheel has literally moved humans out of the ancient world and into modern civilization. Its circular shape and rotating motion continue to play a key role in new ideas and inventions. It has helped to shape the history of exploration and discovery, agriculture and industrialization, travel and entertainment, and electronic and digital forms of communication.

WHAT IF?

Without the wheel, we would not have the technology for transportation, machines, and industries that give us modern conveniences and comforts. And, without the wheel, very few of the life-changing inventions in this book would have been possible.

Quick Fact

The first Ferris wheel was invented in 1893. It was 26 stories high, had a circumference of 823 feet, and was supported by steel towers that rose 144 feet above the ground.

WHAT NOW?

In the early days, carts and wagons made it possible to transport goods over long distances. This led to the building of roads, which gave humans access to more space and allowed for the growth of cities. Today, wheels are functional as well as cool (think Porsche and Lamborghini!). It is safe to say that the simple yet revolutionary technology of the wheel will be around for another few thousand years — it would be impossible to imagine life without it.

?
The wheel is a main feature of transportation vehicles. How have these changed over the years? Create a timeline poster using pictures and captions.

Experts believe that a wheel was used in ancient potters' whe... long before it was e... used to move things

The Expert Says...

" The importance of the wheel's discovery was such that no historian would be far wrong in claiming that the world began moving toward its present civilization on Sumerian wheels. "

— *Saudi Aramco World* (February 1961)

?
Many of the ancient inventions in this book are credited to people who lived in Mesopotamia. Why do you think so many things were invented there?

Check out this report to find out how the wheels on your car could look in the future.

Reinventing the Wheel

Michelin press release:
DETROIT, Michigan, January 9, 2005

Today at the North American International Auto Show (NAIAS) Michelin showcased a potential future for mobility, an integrated tire and wheel combination missing one ingredient that is vital for traditional tire performance ... air. ...

Michelin's Tweel® device is in production and available as an enhancement for future iBOT™ mobility systems. Invented by Dean Kamen, the iBOT™ mobility device has the ability to climb stairs and navigate uneven terrain, offering mobility freedom impossible with traditional wheelchairs. ...

The heart of Tweel® device innovation is its deceptively simple looking hub and spoke design that replaces the need for air pressure while delivering performance previously only available from regular tires. The flexible spokes are fused with a flexible wheel that deforms to absorb shock and rebounds with unimaginable ease. ...

Michelin has also found that it can tune Tweel® device performances independently of each other, which is a significant change from conventional tires. This means that vertical stiffness (which primarily affects ride comfort) and lateral stiffness (which affects handling and cornering) can both be optimized, pushing the performance envelope in these applications and enabling new performances not possible for current inflated tires.

In the future, Tweel® device may reinvent the way that vehicles move. Checking tire pressure, fixing flats, highway blowouts, and balancing between traction and comfort could all fade into memory.

Above: The Tweel® device is used on this iBOT™ mobility device. Together they offer more freedom than a regular wheelchair. Below: The Michelin Tweel® device

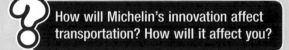

? How will Michelin's innovation affect transportation? How will it affect you?

integrated: *two or more parts combined to form one unit*
hub: *central part of a wheel*

Take Note

The wheel has changed our lives through the centuries. It has influenced other inventions in history and brought about economic, scientific, and technological advancements. Without it, we wouldn't have the computer, pasteurization, television, the steam engine, and the printing press — other outstanding inventions on our list. The wheel (along with its concept) remains an important part of all moving objects today and will likely stay that way.
• Make a list of things you own that involve the technology of the wheel. Beside each item, describe the part it plays in your life.

We Thought ...

Here are the criteria we used in ranking the 10 most revolutionary inventions.

The invention:
- Improved and revolutionized the way we live
- Propelled civilization from a hunting-gathering society to modern age
- Led to other ideas and inventions
- Influenced how people see the world
- Enriched our knowledge of space and the universe
- Started a revolution that changed the world
- Enabled new ways of communicating
- Continues to play a role in our lives and shape our future